JUNIOR FIELD GUIDE

PLANTS
OF
NUNAVUT

WRITTEN BY
Carolyn Mallory

ILLUSTRATED BY
Amiel Sandland

TABLE OF CONTENTS

What Is a Plant?

A plant is a living organism that makes its own food. Plants take nutrients and water from the soil. They take carbon dioxide from the air. And then, with energy from the sun, they transform all of these things into sugar that they can eat. This process is called **photosynthesis**.

When plants photosynthesize, they produce oxygen. Plants produce most of the world's oxygen. We need oxygen to breathe. Plants are very important to all life on Earth.

There are over 390 000 species of plants on the planet. But so far, only about 350 flowering plants have been found in Nunavut. The number of plants in the North is limited because of the harsh climate.

Parts of a Plant

The physical characteristics of a plant are:

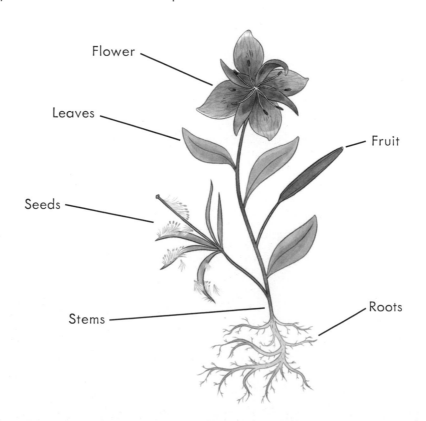

Flower

Leaves

Fruit

Seeds

Stems

Roots

Roots:
The underground roots absorb nutrients and water from the soil. They also anchor the plant in place.

Stems:
The stem acts like a straw. It sucks up the water and nutrients from the roots and sends them to the rest of the plant. Stems also support the above-ground part of the plant so that it does not fall over.

Leaves:
Photosynthesis takes place in the leaves using **chlorophyll**. The leaves also make clean oxygen for us to breathe.

Flowers:
The flowers help the plant **reproduce**. They attract insects to **pollinate** the plant. They produce a fruit.

Fruit:
The fruit protect the seed and help distribute the seeds.

Seeds:
A seed contains all the plant material needed for a new plant to grow. It is protected by a seed coat and also contains some food for the plant to eat before it starts making its own food. Seeds are found inside the fruit.

ALPINE BISTORT

Inuktut: Sapangaralaannguat tuqtaillu

Found
all over
Nunavut

Appearance

Alpine bistort varies a lot in height. It can be anywhere from 2.5 to 24 centimetres high.

The leaves grow mostly at the base of the plant. They are long, thin, and shiny.

Alpine bistort has small pinkish or white flowers that grow in a spike. The flowers on the bottom of the spike open first. **Bulbils** grow along the stem below the flower spike. These bulbils are tiny plant packages. When they drop to the ground, they can grow into new plants.

Alpine bistort plants have a lot going on underground. They have a long, carrot-like root called a **taproot**, and they also have underground stems called **rhizomes**. Rhizomes store food for the winter months.

Range

Alpine bistort is widespread in Nunavut. You should be able to find it in any of the communities.

Growth and Habitat

Bistort is a **perennial**, which means that the leaves and stems die over the winter, but the roots survive underground. The plants grow up from the same roots again in the spring. Because of the rhizomes, and the fact that new plants can grow up from these underground stems, you often see alpine bistort in large groups.

Alpine bistort grows in almost every type of landscape: around ponds, on riverbanks, on the tundra, and even on rocky areas and cliffs.

Adaptations

In the Arctic, alpine bistort rarely produces seeds that can grow into new plants. Instead, the bulbils that drop off the stem can grow into new plants. These new plants are the exact same as the mother plant— clones! The farther north you go, the fewer flowers bistort has, and the higher up on the stem the bulbils appear.

Inuit Knowledge and Uses

The bulbils can be eaten before the flowers develop. They are nutty and crunchy. You could add them to a salad.

The leaves are also edible, but they have an unpleasant texture.

The underground rhizomes get thick in places and can be dug up to eat. They are crunchy and taste like mild almonds. They are starchy and can also be cooked, like tiny potatoes.

Did you know?

Alpine bistort bulbils are eaten by both lemmings and ptarmigans.

ARCTIC COTTON GRASS

Inuktut: Pualunnguat, Kanguujat, Kumaksiutinnguat

Appearance

Arctic cotton grass flowers are most noticeable when they go to seed. That's because each seed is covered by long, fluffy white bristles. Together, all of these bristles make up a flowering head that resembles a round ball of cotton.

The flowering head is on top of a stem that is between 10 and 40 centimetres long. The stem does not have any leaves close to the top. Most of the leaves grow at the bottom of the plant. Each plant has only a few long, narrow leaves.

Arctic cotton grass is not a grass, although its leaves look like grass leaves. It is a type of sedge. Sedges are like grasses but have a different type of seed.

Found all over Nunavut

Range

Arctic cotton grass is found all over Nunavut.

Growth and Habitat

All cotton grasses are perennials. They grow up from the same roots as the year before. Their leaves and stems die over the winter. There are several types of cotton grasses in Nunavut. Look for all of them! Most of them have a single roundish cotton ball, but there is one cotton grass that has several more elongated tufts of cotton on each stem.

Cotton grasses like moist environments. You'll find them in wet meadows, around ponds, lakes, or streams, and in marshes. The plants often grow together in large groups.

Inuit Knowledge and Uses

The cotton can be mixed with moss to make the wick for the **qulliq**.

Arctic cotton grass was used to clean the umbilical cords of newborn babies and to clean cuts. You could also use the cottony tops to clean out an infected ear.

You might also collect enough cotton to put inside a pillow. It could help someone who has a headache to feel better.

Cotton mixed with rancid seal fat can soothe aches and pains.

Did you know?

Muskoxen like to graze on cotton grass!

9

ARCTIC POPPY

Inuktut: Igutsat niqingit

Appearance

Arctic poppies are usually less than 15 centimetres high, but in warmer, sheltered locations, they can be up to 25 centimetres.

When the flowers are in bud, before they open, the stems hang down so that the buds are closer to the ground, where it's warmer. The stems straighten up when the flowers bloom. The bright yellow flowers grow at the top of leafless stems. The flowers have four large petals that fit together to form a bowl shape. Insects are often found warming up in the centre of the flower. Poppies follow the sun as it moves across the sky, keeping their cores warm.

Poppy leaves are very low to the ground, near the base of the plant. They are divided so that one leaf almost looks like more than one. They are also hairy.

Underground, poppies have a long, carrot-like taproot.

Range

There are a few different Arctic poppy species in Nunavut. They are hard to tell apart, even for an expert! They can be found all over Nunavut.

Growth and Habitat

Arctic poppies are perennials. Their leaves and stems die in the winter, but the roots survive underground. In the spring, a new plant grows up in the same spot.

Poppies grow well on disturbed soil, so you will see them around communities by the roadside. They also grow on the tundra, in rocky areas, and near cliffs where birds nest.

Adaptations

Poppy buds are dark and hairy. The dark colour attracts the heat of the sun, and the hair traps that heat to keep the buds warm. The stems are bent so that the buds are close to the ground, where it's even warmer.

Poppies lean toward the sun as it crosses the sky. This keeps the flower warm so that it can grow and reproduce in the cool Arctic summer.

Did you know?

Although most Arctic poppies are bright yellow, you might find some that are greenish, pale yellow, almost white, or even a little pink!

11

ARCTIC THRIFT

Inuktut: Immulik

Appearance

Arctic thrift is easily recognized by its bright pink globe-like flowers. Looking closely, you will see that the flower is actually a group of smaller flowers pressed tightly together.

The flowers grow on leafless stems that are 5 to 20 centimetres high.

All the leaves of Arctic thrift grow in a tuft at the base of the plant. The leaves are fleshy, but long and narrow. They look like grass.

The underground part of the plant is a long, carrot-like taproot.

Range

Arctic thrift is found mostly on mainland Nunavut, all over Baffin Island, on Ellesmere Island, and on some of the other more eastern islands in Nunavut.

Growth and Habitat

Arctic thrift is a perennial, so the leaves and stems die over the winter, but the roots survive underground. In the spring, a new plant grows up from the roots.

Arctic thrift grows in well-drained soils, like sand and gravel. You could also look for it on riverbanks, near beaches, on old lakebeds, and even on the spongy tundra.

Adaptations

Like many plants in the Arctic, thrift has fleshy leaves to help it store water. The lack of rain and snowfall in polar deserts often causes the ground where plants grow to be very dry.

Did you know?

When the Hudson's Bay Company started bringing Carnation evaporated milk to the North, Inuit thought that the flowers on the can looked like Arctic thrift. Inuit then called thrifts "carnations."

13

ARCTIC WHITE HEATHER

Inuktut: Itsutit, Qijuktaat

Appearance

Arctic white heather is a dwarf shrub that grows between 5 and 10 centimetres high—not very tall. Shrubs have many main stems instead of a single trunk like a tree. Arctic white heather shrubs tend to grow in large groups, so you often see many small, white, bell-shaped flowers when they are in bloom. The flowers grow on tiny, curved stalks near the tips of the branches.

The leaves are so tightly pressed against the branches on all four sides that you can't see the branches. They almost look like they are braided.

In the fall, after the flowers are pollinated, the curved stalks straighten up and the fruit develop. The fruit are small, round, orange capsules. They look like tiny pumpkins.

Found all over Nunavut

Range

Arctic white heather is found throughout Nunavut, both on the islands and on the mainland.

Growth and Habitat

Although Arctic white heather is a perennial, it does not lose its leaves in the fall or over the winter like other shrubs. Instead, the leaves turn from bright green to brown. In the spring, they become green again.

These plants prefer north-facing hillsides where they are protected from the winds and where the snow stays late in the spring, giving them a good supply of water to start the growing season. They also commonly grow on the tundra where there is lots of dwarf birch.

Adaptations

The evergreen leaves of Arctic white heather give the plant a head start in the spring. The plant can start photosynthesizing its food as soon as the leaves turn green again.

The leaves are also thick and waxy, to help retain water in the dry Arctic climate.

Inuit Knowledge and Uses

Itsutit, an Inuktut name for the plant, means "fuel for fire." Arctic white heather contains a lot of resin and burns fast and hot.

These small shrubs were often collected for bedding, to make a more comfortable sleeping space. These good-smelling plants must have been nice to sleep on!

Did you know?

Arctic white heather leaves smell beautiful. Next time you're out on the land, give them a sniff!

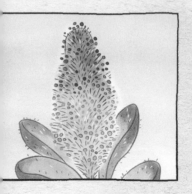

ARCTIC WILLOW

Inuktut: Suputiit, Suputik saliit, Uqaujait

Appearance

Arctic willow is a type of shrub. Like a tree, a shrub is woody, but it has several main stems instead of a single trunk. You can tell how old an Arctic willow is by counting the rings on its woody stem. These willows can be between 3 and 25 centimetres high. They mostly grow along the ground, where it is warmer.

In the summer, Arctic willow leaves are green, but the leaves change colour in the fall and become yellow. The leaves can be many different shapes: narrow, rounded at the ends, egg shaped, or sword shaped. One thing to look for to help you identify Arctic willow is the tuft of long hairs on the underside of the leaf at the tip—kind of like a white beard.

Found all over Nunavut

Range

Arctic willow grows the farthest north of any of the willows. It is very common all over Nunavut.

Arctic willow, like all willows, has separate male and female plants. The flowers on each plant are different. Willow flowers are called catkins. Early in the spring, these catkins are round, soft, and furry. You might know them as pussy willows. Later in the summer, the male catkin has red **anthers**, which hold the pollen. The female flowers have **stigmas**, which look like the letter Y, to receive the pollen. Willows rely mostly on the wind to move the pollen from a male plant to a female plant.

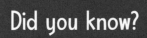

Growth and Habitat

Like most Arctic plants, Arctic willow is a perennial. However, like other tree and shrub species, it loses its leaves before winter. The stems and branches are bare over the winter and grow leaves again in the spring.

Arctic willow is not picky about where it grows. It can be found anywhere from dense tundra to places with very few other plants, and even on cliffs and rocky ridges.

Did you know?

Both muskoxen and Arctic hares eat the leaves and young branches of Arctic willow.

Adaptations

Arctic willow grows along the ground, where it is warmer. There is less wind, and the dark soil attracts the heat of the sun. It can be 20 degrees warmer at ground level. Next time you're out in the summer, try lying down on the tundra to see how much warmer it is at that level!

In the fall, the shrubs produce buds for new leaves before winter sets in. This gives the shrub a bit of a head start in the spring because the leaves are ready to burst as soon as the temperature is warm enough.

Inuit Knowledge and Uses

The leaves of Arctic willow are edible.

People use the top layer of the root to numb tooth aches.

The fluff attached to the seeds, willow cotton, was collected by women to mix with moss to make the wick for the qulliq. Women collected enough cotton and moss to last the whole year.

The willow branches were collected to burn for heat and to use as bedding.

CROWBERRY

Inuktut: Paurngait

Appearance

Crowberry is a dwarf shrub, with many stems instead of a single trunk. The stems grow along the ground, as do most of the branches. These shrubs are less than 15 centimetres tall. The branches and stems can grow in any direction and they get all tangled, forming large crowberry mats.

The tiny leaves of the crowberry are curled under at the edges, making them look very thin. These leaves turn brown in the fall and stay on the plant all winter. They turn green again in the spring.

Crowberry has really small burgundy flowers between the leaves. They bloom very early in the spring, and only for a short time. They are easier to see with a magnifying glass.

At the end of the summer, crowberry plants produce a purplish-black edible fruit. Before the fruit is ripe, it is pale green, then red.

Range

Crowberry is more common in the eastern part of Nunavut than in the western part. You will find it on Baffin Island, Ellesmere Island, and on the mainland.

Growth and Habitat

This perennial grows in the same spot year after year. Its branches, stems, and leaves do not die over the winter.

Crowberry often grows near blueberry plants and Arctic white heather on slopes, gravel, rocks, or dry tundra.

Adaptations

Crowberry stretches out along the ground, where it is warmer, instead of growing upright.

The underside of the leaves is covered with brown hair, like duffle, to keep them warm. The leaves are also thick and waxy to help store water in the dry Arctic climate.

Because the stems and branches get tangled, this plant forms large mats. These mats keep the ground underneath them moister than if the ground was exposed. This again helps the plants to get enough water in the desert-like Arctic.

Inuit Knowledge and Uses

Crowberries are eaten raw. They can be mixed with seal fat to eat or stored in seal fat to keep them fresh.

The leaves and small branches can be boiled to make a tea that helps with diarrhea.

The branches and stems can be collected to make a more comfortable place to sleep.

Crowberries are made into a delicacy by mixing them with shredded caribou fat and seal oil and then eaten like pudding.

Did you know?

Migrating birds flying south often eat many of these berries. Perhaps you've seen purple goose poop? Now you know why!

DWARF FIREWEED

Inuktut: Paunnat

Appearance

Dwarf fireweed have the largest flowers in Nunavut. The flowers have four rounded pink petals. They have four darker purple-pink pointy **sepals**, which you can see between the paler petals. If you look closely when the flower is in full bloom, you will see turquoise pollen on the anthers sticking out in the middle of the flower.

The leaves grow on a floppy stem that is between 5 and 30 centimetres high. The flowers grow on the top of the stem in groups of three to five.

Found all over Nunavut

Range

Whichever community you live in, you will be able to see dwarf fireweed. It grows all over Nunavut and beyond. It's actually the national flower of Greenland!

Dwarf fireweed has horizontal underground stems called rhizomes. They help to store food for the plant. New plants can also grow up from these rhizomes.

The other underground part of the plant is the mass of fibrous roots, kind of like a mop of curly hair, growing beneath the plant.

Growth and Habitat

Dwarf fireweed leaves and stems die over the winter, but the roots survive underground. In the spring, new plants grow up from the roots. This makes dwarf fireweed a perennial. New plants can also grow from the seeds produced in dwarf fireweed's long, pod-like fruit.

These plants grow really well along the sides of roads, beside streams, or on burnt lands. This is because the plants love bare, disturbed soil where there are few other plants to compete with.

Inuit Knowledge and Uses

The leaves, flowers, and seed pods of dwarf fireweed are edible. They are tasty on their own or mixed with fat, blood, or oil. The leaves can also be cooked.

Tea can be made with the leaves to help with stomach aches and to make a person stronger after they have lost a lot of blood. Chewing the leaves can help stop a nosebleed.

Did you know?

Rarely, dwarf fireweed produces white flowers instead of pink. Keep your eyes peeled when you're out for a walk! Some have been seen around Iqaluit and Rankin Inlet.

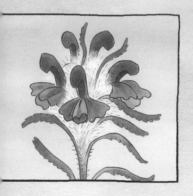

HAIRY LOUSEWORT

Inuktut: Ugjunnait

Appearance

Hairy lousewort has small pink flowers that grow clumped around a central hairy stem. The flowers each have five petals. The top two petals are combined to form what looks like a helmet. The other three petals are more open so that insects can crawl in. Insects are needed to pollinate the flowers.

The leaves grow along the stem in between the flowers and in a tuft at the base of the plant. In early spring, before the flowers come out, people often mistake the plants for ferns because their leaves are divided and frilly. The leaves growing up the stems are much less divided.

Range

Hairy lousewort has been found all over the Nunavut mainland and most of the islands, except for Victoria Island and Prince of Wales Island, where there are no records of it yet.

These plants grow between 5 and 15 centimetres high. The plants get taller as the flowers open up. They get even taller when the flowers go to seed. The seeds are blown out of the fruit capsule when they are ripe. If the plant is taller when this happens, then the seeds can be blown farther away. This is healthy for all the plants because if they are spread out, they will not have to compete for the same water or food.

The underground part of this plant is a long, carrot-like taproot.

Growth and Habitat

Like all louseworts, hairy lousewort is a perennial. The roots survive the winter, but the above-ground parts die off and come up again the following spring.

Hairy lousewort grows in all sorts of different habitats: damp rocky tundra, riverbanks, lakeshores, cliffs, gravel, sand, and even in **peat**.

Inuit Knowledge and Uses

The stems and leaves can be cooked in a soup or stew. Roots and young stems can be eaten raw.

Did you know?

If you cut one of the flowers in half horizontally right down the middle, the two sides are mirror images. This is called bilateral symmetry.

23

Mountain Avens

Inuktut: Malikkaat

Found
all over
Nunavut

Appearance

Mountain avens are dwarf shrubs. These shrubs are very tiny, usually less than 15 centimetres tall. Their short stems produce branches that lie flat on the ground, and because they grow in all directions, these branches can get tangled and form mats that cover large areas.

The plant's pale yellow blossoms grow at the top of a long, reddish, leafless stalk. The flowers have between 7 and 11 egg-shaped petals. In the centre of the flowers, you can see many bright yellow anthers, which hold the pollen.

The tiny, arrow-shaped leaves feel leathery to the touch. They are a beautiful dark green in the summer and change to yellow and orange in the fall.

Range

Mountain avens are very widespread in Nunavut. You will be able to find some wherever you live.

Growth and Habitat

Although its stems don't die over the winter, mountain avens are still perennials. The leaves die at the end of the fall season, but they stay attached to the branches to protect them over the winter and to keep the buds warm in the spring.

Mountain avens grow mostly in drier areas, whether it be on the tundra or on rocks, clay, ridges, or old riverbeds.

Adaptations

Like Arctic poppies, mountain avens lean toward the sun as it crosses the sky. This keeps the centre of the flower, where the reproductive parts are, warm. It also provides a warm place for insects to rest, which encourages pollination.

Like most Arctic plants, the stems, branches, and leaves grow very close to the ground, where it is warmer.

The leaves have very hairy undersides like duffle to help trap the heat and keep the leaves warm.

Dark, hairy buds keep the reproductive parts warm before the flowers bloom. The dark colour attracts the heat of the sun, and the hairs trap that heat.

Inuit Knowledge and Uses

The Inuktut name for mountain avens is *malikkaat,* which means "follower."

Mountain avens can be thought of as a calendar. It's summer when they begin to bloom, and then they change to long strands coiled together as the seeds form in full summer. As autumn approaches, the strands uncoil and the seeds get ready to be blown away.

Did you know?

Before they are ripe, the seeds are important food for birds and small mammals.

MOUNTAIN SORREL

Inuktut: Qunguliit

Appearance

Mountain sorrel has bright green, kidney-shaped leaves that are often outlined in red. The leaves are on long stalks and grow in a clump at the base of the plant.

The flowering stems are bright red and much taller than the leaves. The flowers are not really flower-like—that is, they don't have any petals. The flowers look like dangly beads. They can be red, pink, white, or even semi-transparent.

Underground stems, or rhizomes, allow the plants to grow in large groups. New plants can grow up from these underground stems just a little way from the original plant. When new plants grow up at regular intervals, this makes for a lot of mountain sorrel in one place. Mountain sorrel also has a long, carrot-like taproot.

Found
all over
Nunavut

Range

Mountain sorrel is very common all over the Arctic islands and on the mainland in Nunavut.

Growth and Habitat

These plants are perennials, and all of the leaves and stems die over the winter. A new plant grows up from the roots in the springtime.

Mountain sorrel can grow in a number of different habitats: near communities or cliffs where birds nest, on snowbed slopes, and in wet gravel or on **hummocky** tundra. Snowbed slopes are slopes that, because of the direction they face, accumulate snow until late in the spring. The plants that grow there have plenty of water from the late melting snow.

Inuit Knowledge and Uses

Because few fruits and even fewer vegetables grow on the land, mountain sorrel was an important source of vitamin C. The leaves, flowers, and seeds can be eaten raw for that sweet and sour taste or boiled for a milder flavour. The roots are only eaten raw.

Because mountain sorrel makes you salivate when you eat it raw, it can help to quench your thirst when you are walking on the land.

Medicinally, the leaves can be boiled to ease a stomach ache or to help people who have low energy.

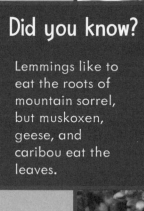

Did you know?

Lemmings like to eat the roots of mountain sorrel, but muskoxen, geese, and caribou eat the leaves.

27

PURPLE SAXIFRAGE

Inuktut: Aupilattunnguat

Found
all over
Nunavut

Appearance

Purple saxifrage plants do not grow very tall, only between 2 and 5 centimetres. The plants can look quite different depending on where they are growing. Sometimes they are even hard to recognize. They can be very tiny with all the leaves tightly packed together in very windy, dry places. In other places, they can grow trailing down a rock face, and the leaves are more spread apart on long stems. Or, they can grow in mounds called cushions where you can't see any of the branches because they are all underneath the tightly packed leaves. And in some places, they grow into very large mats, making the whole plant seem huge!

Range

Purple saxifrage is one of the first plants to bloom in the spring all over Nunavut.

The leaves are very small, thick, and waxy. They are triangular and grow in pairs on opposite sides of the stems. The second pair of triangular leaves grows at 90 degrees to the first pair. So, four leaves together form a square shape on the stem.

The purple flowers have five petals and are much, much bigger than the leaves. However, they are still small flowers.

The root is a long, carrot-like taproot.

Did you know?

Purple saxifrage is one of only four plants that grow in the most northern location on Earth!

Growth and Habitat

Purple saxifrage is a perennial that grows up from the same spot every spring. Its branches become woody and new growth occurs at the tips of the branches. The woody parts do not die over the winter, and some of the leaves also stay on the plant.

These plants grow everywhere! You can find purple saxifrage in wet or dry areas, on the tundra, on rocks and gravel, along streams, or even in the most unlikely places where nothing else grows. This is likely why it was chosen as the territorial flower of Nunavut. It loves harsh environments with no other competition.

Adaptations

Purple saxifrage can form cushions if the environment is very harsh. In cushion plants, the stems and branches are packed tightly under the leaves, and the whole plant forms a mound that the wind blows over instead of through. This protects the whole plant from damage. This type of cushion is also warmer because it's pressed close to the ground. It keeps the soil underneath wetter.

The leaves of the plant are thick and waxy to preserve water in the Arctic's desert-like climate.

Inuit Knowledge and Uses

The flowers are tasty, especially when mixed with seal fat or blubber.

Tea can be made from the leaves.

Glossary

anther: the part of a flower that produces and contains pollen.

bulbils: tiny plant packages that arise on a plant's stem. When they drop to the ground, they can grow into new plants that are clones (exact copies) of the mother plant.

chlorophyll: a green pigment found in most plants that allows plants to absorb and use light to provide energy for photosynthesis.

hummocky: land that contains humps or ridges formed by the freezing and thawing of the ground.

peat: blackish or dark brown material composed of decayed plants that is formed in swamps or bogs.

perennial: a plant that grows for many growing seasons. The leaves and stems usually die over the winter, but the roots survive underground. In the spring, a new plant grows up from the roots. If the perennial is a shrub, then the branches and stems survive the winter and the leaves grow again in the spring. Some leaves also stay on the plants all winter, becoming dormant and brown in the winter and greening up again in the spring.

photosynthesis: the process through which plants produce their own food using nutrients and water from the soil, carbon dioxide from the air, and energy from the sun that is absorbed by the plant's chlorophyll.

pollination: the process of pollen being transferred from the anther to the stigma that allows plants to produce fruit and seeds.

qulliq: traditional oil lamp used by Inuit. The lamp was traditionally made of stone, filled with fat from animals such as seals and whales, and lit using a wick made of Arctic cotton grass or Arctic willow mixed with moss.

reproduce: to produce new plants of the same species through seeds or bulbils.

rhizomes: underground stems that usually grow horizontally. They help to store food for the plant, and new plants can also grow up from them.

sepal: part of a flower that usually protects the flower when it is a bud and supports the petal when it blooms.

stigma: the part of a flower that receives the pollen.

taproot: a long, carrot-like root that grows straight down.

INHABIT
EDUCATION
BOOKS